A CALL TO ACTION

A Companion Guide to the Steward Declaration

Andrea Capuyan | Ben Porter |
Howard Rich | and Brian Simmons

KINGDOM LIFE PUBLISHING

A CALL TO ACTION:
A Companion Guide to the Steward Declaration

Copyright © 2023 by Kingdom Life Publishing

All rights reserved under International and Pan-American Copyright Conventions. Reproductions or translation of any part of this work beyond that permitted by section 107 or 108 of the 1976 United States Copyright Act is unlawful.

Requests for permissions should be addressed to:
Kingdom Life Publishing
P.O. Box 389
Colbert, WA 99005

To contact the authors, write to:
publisher@kingdomlifepublishing.com

U.S.A.

All Scripture quotations, unless otherwise indicated, are taken from the Holy Bible, New International Version, NIV. Copyright © 1973, 1978, 1984 by International Bible Society. All rights reserved.

ISBN 978-1-7362697-4-9
Printed in the United States of America

CONTENTS

PREFACE 1

INTRODUCTION 5

OUR RELATIONSHIP WITH GOD 9

OUR RELATIONSHIP WITH SELF 27

OUR RELATIONSHIP WITH OTHERS 37

OUR RELATIONSHIP WITH CREATION 49

CONCLUSION 59

REFERENCES 61

ABOUT THE AUTHORS 63

ABOUT THE EDITOR 69

PREFACE

Dr. Scott Rodin

In Daniel chapter 3, we read the familiar story of Shadrach, Meshach, Abednego, and the fiery furnace. Most often, when this story is shared, the focus is on the miraculous rescue of the three from the blazing inferno.

As we consider our response to the challenges facing our country and our world, I want to focus on a different part of the story and its impact on the decisions we make. To me, the most challenging part of the drama is the command from King Nebuchadnezzar for all people to "fall down" on their faces and worship the idol he had created once they heard his music playing (Dan. 3:4–5). It seems there were two purposes for this. The first was to ensure that homage was being paid by all the citizens of the land. The second was to clearly identify any recusants.

What might we have done if given such a choice? As our American culture continues its rapid moral decline, the values of the kingdom of God and its central

A CALL TO ACTION

messages of sin, grace, salvation, sacrifice, and obedience are standing out in the starkest contrast against a background of narcissism and human avarice—so much so that we are considered anathema to those bent on driving the Christian message from all public life.

The increasing acrimony toward the Christian message is a modern version of the king's music, heard through the power of intimidation, social media threats, ostracization, and condemnation. When it plays, how do we respond? Do we stand firm, burned in the fire of public disapproval? Or do we bow down and let our silence save us?

I wonder if we as evangelicals in America are choosing a third option, or at least attempting it. While it's easy to say we will stand firm and face the flames of an increasingly hostile culture, I wonder if, too often, we try to find a middle ground.

In Daniel's day, as the music started playing, imagine if Shadrach, Meshach, and Abednego had responded by bending over just enough to appear to the authorities to be bowing down, in order to save them from the furnace, while also seeming to be standing up just enough to not forsake their faith. What a sad scene!

The three would have nothing to do with such a compromise. They stood tall for all to see. Their faith reflected Jesus's later command: "You will be hated by everyone because of me, but the one who stands firm to the end will be saved" (Matt. 10:22).

Yet despite Jesus's command to stand firm, and the

PREFACE

witness of Shadrach, Meshach, and Abednego, it seems this kind of crouching Christianity is a choice we too easily make even as we desire to be faithful Jesus-followers. In the face of growing hostility to our faith, we can easily forget that Jesus's invitation to follow him includes his command that we must take up our cross in order to do so (Luke 9:23).

My question for us is this: Will we stand tall in our day when our culture plays its music and demands we compromise our values, conform to the standards of this world, and accommodate, or at least privatize, our faith? Will we be crouching Christians, or will we, like our three friends in the book of Daniel, stand firm regardless of the cost?

What might it look like to stand tall in our current cultural chaos? Well, here is one option right before us.

On Epiphany, January 6, we officially launched *The Steward Declaration*. This is a product of a group of about thirty people who met annually for the last eight years to present papers and dialogue on issues of faith and the life of the faithful steward. From those summits we produced a document that is our attempt to proclaim the truth and call the body of Christ in America back to the fully surrendered, obedient, and joyful life of the faithful steward.

What follows is a series of reflections on that document, helping readers go deeper in their understanding and embrace the implications of this steward theology. This is a call to action to the body of Christ!

A CALL TO ACTION

You are invited to take up this call and sign and share *The Steward Declaration*. By adding your name to this declaration, you will join the growing movement of God's people who are standing firm and proclaiming truth regardless of the cost.

Let's come together and send a message to our nation that God's people take their faith seriously and will live boldly according to kingdom values. May this Call to Action encourage and bless you on your steward journey.

Read and sign the Steward Declaration at
www.thestewarddeclaration.com

INTRODUCTION

What is a servant leader? Greenleaf (1977) emphasized the motives and heart of the leader, asserting that a servant leader is "servant first." He shared, "It begins with the natural feeling that one wants to serve, to serve first. The conscious choice brings one to aspire to lead." He continued, "The difference manifests itself in the care taken by the servant-first to make sure that other people's highest priority needs are being served" (7). In the late 1980s, another leader, Max De Pree, defined servant leadership as "the process of removing obstacles that prevent others from doing their jobs and enabling followers to realize their full potential," noting that a "true leader is a listener who, within the context of his own beliefs, responds appropriately" (as cited in Wilson 2016, 47).

What is a steward? Birch (2002) defined a steward as "one who has the responsibility for the care and use of resources that belong to another" (358). Wilson (2016) defined a steward as "anyone who manages property and

A CALL TO ACTION

resources belonging to another in order to achieve the owner's objectives" (85). Rodin (2013) noted that leaders under this model must be stewards of relationships on four levels: relationship with God, relationship with self, relationship with our neighbor, and relationship with creation. These four categories provide the four chapters for this *Steward Leader Declaration: A Call to Action*.

So what is a steward leader? "Steward leaders empower their people, give away authority, value and involve others, seek the best in and from their people, and constantly lift others up, push others into the limelight and reward those they lead—all so that God's will may be done in a more powerful way. They seek no glory for themselves, but find great joy in seeing others prosper. They take no account of their reputation, but desire that Jesus's face be seen in all they do" (Rodin 2002, 7). Block (2013) elaborated, "The spirit of stewardship demands a conversation on institutional purpose and how it cares for the common good" (251).

One of the key concepts that differentiate steward and servant leadership is that all stewards are servants, but not all servants are stewards (Wilson 2016). Wilson defined steward leadership as "the efficient management and growth of organizational resources, through leadership of staff and activities as a non-owning steward–servant, in order to achieve the mission according to the objectives of the owners" (34). So the steward leader construct adds a vertical relational dimension to the horizontal relationships defined by the servant leader model.

INTRODUCTION

Finally, the steward leader model adds an organizational dimension, as "only steward leadership addresses all of the resources that must be managed, the steward's relationship with those resources and the intended outcome of resource management" (49). A steward leader's faithful devotion to a growing relationship with God, Who is the Creator and ultimate "Owner" of everyone and everything, is foundational to effective leadership. In short, a faithful steward leader loves and serves God by loving and serving others.

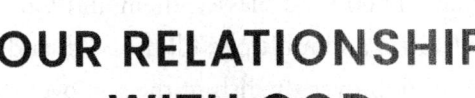

OUR RELATIONSHIP WITH GOD

Dr. Brian S. Simmons

Let us then approach God's throne of grace with confidence, so that we may receive mercy and find grace to help us in our time of need.

—Hebrews 4:16

What We Believe about the Stewardship of Our Relationship with God

We were created to be faithful stewards, starting with our relationship with God. "In the beginning, God created the heavens and the earth" (Gen. 1:1). "Then God said, let us make man in Our image, according to Our likeness; let them have dominion over the fish of the sea, over the birds of the air, and over the cattle, over all the earth, and over every creeping thing that creeps on the earth. So God created man in His own image, in

A CALL TO ACTION

the image of God He created him; male and female He created them. Then God blessed them and God said to them, 'Be fruitful and multiply; fill the earth and subdue it; have dominion over the fish of the sea, over the birds of the air, and over every living thing that moves on the earth'" (Gen. 1:26–28). "The image of God in humanity, or the *imago Dei*, has been extensively interpreted by theologians and relates directly to people as stewards of God. In the ancient Near East, a king would sometimes erect an image of himself in a territory as a symbol of his sovereignty. In a similar vein, humans can be seen as God's representatives on earth since they bear God's image" (Wilson 2016, 52).

"The earth is the Lord's and everything in it. The world and all its people belong to Him" (Ps. 24:1). From these passages of Scripture, we learn that God is the Creator. As Creator, He alone retains the rights of ownership over all He has created. Stewards, then, do not live in the realm of rights. Stewards live in the realm of responsibility as caretakers or managers for all that belongs to the Master. Wilson (2016) applied this to organizational leadership when he wrote, "Steward leadership is the efficient management and growth of organizational resources, through leadership staff and activities, as a non-owning steward–servant in order to achieve the mission according to the objectives of the owner" (86).

Sometime after creation, the fall occurred (Gen. 3). Adam and Eve sinned, their relationship with God was broken, and they were removed from the Garden of

OUR RELATIONSHIP WITH GOD

Eden (Gen. 3:24). The remainder of the Bible is about Jesus Christ and God's plan for redemption. God's plan of salvation, the gospel, can be summarized by one of the most beloved verses in all of Scripture: "For God so loved the world that He gave His only begotten Son that whosoever believeth in Him shall not perish but shall have everlasting life" (John 3:16). To place one's faith in Jesus Christ is to become a follower of Christ—a Christian. Accepting Christ as one's personal Lord and Savior is the point at which a personal relationship with God begins. Faithful stewards are committed to growing in this precious relationship with God through Jesus Christ that has been entrusted to their care.

"Oh, the depth of the riches of the wisdom and knowledge of God! How unsearchable His judgments and His paths beyond tracing out. Who has known the mind of the Lord? Or who has been His counselor? Who has ever given to God, that God should repay them? For from Him and through Him and for Him are all things. To Him be the glory forever! Amen" (Rom. 11:33–36). All things are *from Him, through Him, and for Him*!

All things, including our relationships with others, are from Him. This reminds me of the time a few years ago when I accepted the call to become the president of the Association of Christian Schools International (ASCI). The ACSI headquarters is located in Colorado Springs, Colorado, so my family and I were preparing for a long move from Indiana. The week of our move, my youngest daughter, Aubrey, was in downtown Indianapolis

A CALL TO ACTION

spending a few final hours with friends. My phone rang a little after midnight while I was crawling into bed. It was Aubrey. She said, "Dad, which way do I go on Interstate 70 to get home?" just as I heard a loud *CRASH*, and the phone went dead. I leaped out of bed, pulled on my shorts, and raced downstairs to drive downtown, when the phone rang again. It was Aubrey, and she said, "Dad, I'm okay, but your Durango..." As I drove downtown, I thought, the Durango is God's. We can buy another vehicle. Then the thought hit me that Aubrey is also God's, and He has entrusted my *relationship* with her to me as her father for a finite period of time! All things, including the people we love, are *from* Him!

All things are also *through* Him. Biblical stewards understand that all the good works we do are enabled by Him. While living in Colorado Springs, I had the distinct privilege of meeting occasionally with author Jerry Bridges. In his book, *The Pursuit of Holiness*, Bridges (1978) explained what he called the divine/human cooperative. In short, God *enables all we do* and *does what only He can do*! As stewards, we manage the tension between "let go and let God" on one end of the continuum, and "just do it" on the other. Bridges explained this divine/human cooperative further in the preface to his book:

A farmer plants his field, sows the seed, and fertilizes and cultivates—all the while knowing that in the final analysis he is utterly dependent on forces outside of himself. He knows he cannot cause the seed to germinate, nor can he produce the rain and sunshine for growing

OUR RELATIONSHIP WITH GOD

and harvesting the crop. For a successful harvest, he is dependent on these things from God. Yet the farmer knows that unless he diligently pursues his responsibilities to plow, plant, fertilize and cultivate, he cannot expect a harvest at the end of the season. In a sense he is in a partnership with God, and he will reap its benefits only when he has fulfilled his own responsibilities (9).

So all things are *through* Him.

Lastly, all things are *for* Him. According to the *Westminster Catechism* (1647), the chief end of man is to glorify God and to enjoy Him forever. God alone, as Creator, lives in the realm of rights. As Creator of all, He retains the rights of ownership for everything He has created. Stewards live in the realm of responsibilities. When we think, "That's not right; that's not fair," or "I want my rights, my will, my way," we are embracing an ownership mentality. As God's stewards, we are to faithfully use all that He has *so graciously* entrusted to our care to fulfill His purposes for His glory!

"*Therefore*, I urge you, brothers and sisters, in view of God's mercy, *to offer your bodies as a living sacrifice*, holy and pleasing to God—this is your reasonable act of worship. Do not conform to the pattern of this world, but be transformed by the renewing of your mind. Then you will be able to test and approve what God's will is—His good, pleasing and perfect will" (Rom. 12:1–2; emphasis added). Following Jesus in our day and in this culture will look nothing like it did in the past. For us to faithfully follow our Lord into the world will require

A CALL TO ACTION

us to steward our identity through a passionate return to the kind of *complete surrender* that leads to freedom and the peace of God that surpasses all understanding. Only by giving up control, trusting the Holy Spirit, living in moment-by-moment obedience, *surrendering* the outcomes, and waiting on God will true revival come. *The way up is by getting down on our knees, daily surrendering our will to His!* This is countercultural. But we ought to say, "Lord, today I want to go Your way."

I suggest this daily prayer of submission: "Lord, I want to do Your will. I submit myself to You today. I want to love and serve You by loving and serving others. I want to put service over self-interest today. Please keep me from the traps, snares, and pitfalls of the evil one and help me to faithfully fulfill Your purposes for all You have *so graciously* entrusted to my care! I ask this in Jesus's name. Amen." The faithful steward is motivated by a heart of gratitude for all God has graciously done for and entrusted to him.

The Apostle Paul wrote to the believers in Ephesus:

> Therefore, I also, after I heard of your faith in the Lord Jesus and your love for all the saints, do not cease to give thanks for you, making mention of you in my prayers: that the God of our Lord Jesus Christ, the Father of glory, may give to you the spirit of wisdom and revelation in the knowledge of Him, the eyes of your understanding being enlightened; *that you may know what*

is the hope of His calling, what are the riches of the glory of His inheritance in the saints, and what is the exceeding greatness of His power toward us who believe, according to the working of His mighty power which He worked in Christ Jesus when He raised Him from the dead and seated Him at His right hand in the heavenly places, far above all principality and power and might and dominion, and every name that is named, not only in this age but also in that which is to come. And He put all things under His feet, and gave Him to be head over all things to the church, which is His body, the fullness of Him who fills all in all (Eph. 1:15–22; emphasis added).

Followers of Jesus Christ, like Jesus, are stewards of God the Father. Jesus said of His purpose in coming to earth, "For I have come down from heaven, not to do my own will, but to *do the will of Him who sent me*" (John 6:38; emphasis added). As God's stewards, we are entrusted by the Father with time, treasure, talents, and relationships. Of these, the most precious gift is relationships, beginning with believers' vertical relationship with God! We know this because going back to creation, after God created the universe, earth, plants, and animals, "God saw that it was *good*" (Gen. 1:25; emphasis added). Then God created man, and "God saw everything He had made, and indeed it was *very good*" (Gen. 1:31; emphasis added)! Of all of creation, only mankind

A CALL TO ACTION

is created in the image of God. So as stewards of our relationship with God, we are to seek His will for all He has so graciously entrusted to our care. And the greatest of these gifts is relationships.

While on earth, Jesus was asked, "Teacher, which is the greatest commandment in the Law?" Jesus replied, "Love the Lord your God with all your heart and with all your soul and with all your mind. This is the first and greatest commandment. And the second is like it: 'Love your neighbor as yourself.' All the Law and the Prophets hang on these two commandments" (Matt. 22:36–40). So as stewards of our relationship with God, we are to love Him above all else! As the steward's vertical relationship with God grows stronger and stronger, the faithful steward also demonstrates a growing love for God by developing horizontal relationships with others. In other words, the faithful steward loves and serves God by loving and serving others.

Stewards do not own relationships with God and others but instead steward them on behalf of the owner (God). Stewards, by definition, are ones to whom a trust has been given. A trust is an arrangement whereby one (a trustee or steward) manages time, treasure, talents, and relationships for another (the owner). So stewards do not own these relationships—the Creator does! In other words, God alone retains the rights of ownership and has the sole prerogative for all He has created.

It follows, then, that the purpose for our lives and the meaning of our existence is discovered solely in a

OUR RELATIONSHIP WITH GOD

deepening, intimate relationship with God through Jesus Christ. As His stewards, we find meaning and purpose in life as we seek to fulfill His purposes for all that He has so graciously entrusted to our care. This is a biblical calling. The root word in Latin for calling is *vocare*. From *vocare* comes the English word *vocation*. So biblical stewards find their calling—their meaning and purpose in life—as they seek the will of the Creator for the time, treasures, talents, and especially relationships entrusted to their care in each of their vocational realms. These vocational *realms* parallel the steward's life *roles*. As an example, the role of a Christian is to be a follower of Jesus Christ. Therefore, biblical stewards find deep meaning and fulfillment in life as they develop a strong relationship with their Creator, God, made possible through personal faith in Jesus Christ!

Gene Edward Veith Jr. (2002) expanded on this theme:

> When we pray the Lord's Prayer…we ask God to give us this day our daily bread…He does it by means of the farmer who planted and harvested the grain, the baker who made the flour into bread, the person who prepared our meal. We might today add the truck drivers who hauled the produce, the factory workers in the food processing plant, the warehouse men, the wholesale distributors, the stock boys, the lady at the checkout counter. Also playing their part

A CALL TO ACTION

are the bankers, future investors, advertisers, lawyers, agricultural scientists, mechanical engineers, and every other player in the nation's economic system. *All of these were instrumental in enabling you to eat your morning bagel* (13; emphasis added).

This explains the Christian steward's calling in the world! This broadened biblical understanding of stewardship brings meaning and purpose to life. "God has chosen to work through human beings, who, in their different capacities (vocational realms/stewardship roles) and according to their different talents, serve each other. This is the doctrine of vocation" (Veith 2002, 13–14). Further, there is no secular (without God)/sacred divide for the faithful steward because all of life is sacred and every life decision is a stewardship decision!

When we embrace our call to steward our relationship with God, we can experience true intimacy with Him. What does this "embracing" look like? When I turned sixteen, my dad gave me a Bible. In the front cover he wrote, "Son. This book will keep you from sin. Sin will keep you from this book." Then he wrote Joshua 1:8: "This book of the law shall not depart out of thy mouth; but thou shalt meditate therein day and night, that thou mayest observe to do according to all that is written therein. For then thou shalt make thy way prosperous, and then thou shalt have good success."

For followers of Christ, this deepening, loving rela-

OUR RELATIONSHIP WITH GOD

tionship is developed by practicing the spiritual disciplines, such as Scripture reading, prayer, meditation, fasting, and service, which is living in obedience to the will of God. As we care for the depth of our walk with God, He cares for the breadth of our impact and ministry. But as Howard Hendricks (2003) famously said, "We cannot take people where we have not been or are unwilling to go ourselves, and we cannot impart what we do not possess." Hendricks continued, "Teaching that impacts is not head to head, but heart to heart…to the Hebrews, heart embraced the totality of human personality—one's intellect, one's emotions and one's will" (105). The faithful steward loves the Lord with all his heart!

Biblical stewards grow to become fully prepared, devoted followers of Jesus Christ.

> Knowing that a man is not justified by the works of the law but by faith in Jesus Christ, even we have believed in Christ Jesus that we might be justified by faith in Christ and not by the works of the law; for by the works of the law no flesh shall be justified. But if, while we seek to be justified by Christ, we ourselves are found sinners, is Christ therefore a minister of sin? Certainly not! For if I build again those things which I destroyed, I make myself a transgressor. For I through the law have died to the law that I might live to God. I have been crucified with Christ; it is no longer I who live, but Christ lives in me;

and the life I now live in the flesh I live by faith in the Son of God who loved me and gave Himself for me" (Gal. 2:16–20).

In his book *The Divine Conspiracy: Rediscovering Our Hidden Life in God*, Dallas Willard (1998) stated that biblical stewards pass through a "course of training" as they grow from "their faith in Christ to having the faith of Christ!" The first step in this course of training is to bring the steward to the place where they "clearly love and constantly delight in that 'heavenly father' made real to earth in Jesus, and are quite certain there is no 'catch' no limit to the goodness of his intentions or his power to carry them out" (321). And the second objective of a curriculum for Christlikeness is "to remove our automatic responses against the kingdom of God to free the stewards of domination, of 'enslavement'" (322). "Jesus answered them, 'Most assuredly, I say to you, whoever commits sin is a slave of sin'" (John 8:34). "Knowing this, that our old man was crucified with Christ, that the body of sin might be done away with, that we should no longer be slaves to sin" (Rom. 6:6). Biblical stewards recognize that while they may still struggle with propensity to sin in the flesh, the power of sin over them has been broken by Christ!

In his book *The Normal Christian Life*, Watchman Nee (1957) posed the question, "What is the normal Christian life? We do well at the outset to ponder this question. The object of these studies is to show that it is something very different from the life of the average

OUR RELATIONSHIP WITH GOD

Christian. Indeed, a consideration of the written Word of God—of the Sermon on the mount for example—should lead us to ask whether such a life has ever in fact been lived upon the earth, *save only by the Son of God himself.* But in that last saving clause lies immediately the answer to our question" (11). Additionally, Nee said that faithful stewards realize that the perfect life of Christ has been imputed to their account, and that in this truth lies the answer to the question! Through faith, the faithful steward knows the truth of the gospel and more specifically that he is dead to sin, reckons this as true in his life, and yields himself to Christ through daily surrender of his will to the will of his Father, God. This daily knowing, reckoning, and yielding deepens the steward's relationship with his loving Heavenly Father (Rom. 6)!

When we do not embrace our call to steward our relationship with God, we allow distractions to steal the joy of this intimacy and lure us into a two-kingdom life where we try to serve two masters. Either we place God on the throne of our lives, or we place ourselves there. There is no middle ground! "No one can serve two masters, for either he will hate the one and love the other, or he will be devoted to the one and despise the other. You cannot serve God and money" (Matt. 6:24). How does this fit with biblical stewardship? The biblical steward understands that his money, in fact his entire life, is not his own! God owns it all! "For you are bought with a price; therefore glorify God in your body" (1 Cor. 6:20). So the biblical steward chooses to love God and use his

A CALL TO ACTION

time, treasure, talent, and entire life, entrusted by God to his care, to accomplish the purposes of the Master instead of his own selfish desires. The unfaithful steward loves his time, his talent, and his money and tries to use God. One path leads to deep purpose and fulfillment, and the other ends in death, which is separation from God and His purposes for all eternity.

Therefore, biblical stewards reject the lie that there are things in this world that can bring more pleasure, happiness, and peace than knowing God intimately. Biblical stewards reject the lie that human beings can own and control their relationship with God and conform this relationship to ways they believe will bring the most happiness. And biblical stewards reject the deceptive lie that anyone can experience intimacy with Christ apart from confession, repentance, surrender, and obedience. The biblical steward understands that "the way up" is "down on his knees" in daily surrender to the will of the Master. Finally, biblical stewards reject the lie that God is more concerned with what we do than who we are, that working for God should be more valued than letting God work in us, and that producing fruit through our labor is a higher calling than bearing the fruit of the Spirit through abiding in Christ.

Biblical Stewards Are Committed to Proclaiming the Truth of the Gospel

As stewards, we embrace the truth that God's heart is rooted in a love so lavish that He sent His own Son for

OUR RELATIONSHIP WITH GOD

the purpose of redeeming our lives, forgiving our sin, and drawing us close to Himself. "For God so loved the world that He sent His only begotten Son that whosoever believeth in Him shall not perish but shall have everlasting life" (John 3:16). This reminds me of our mission at Columbia International University where I serve as associate provost and professor for CIU Global. Our mission states that "CIU educates students from a biblical worldview to impact the nations with the message of Christ." In his book *We Will Not Be Silenced: Responding with Courage to Our Culture's Assault on Christianity*, Erwin Lutzer (2020) wrote that as Christians living as biblical stewards, we should not be silenced by this assault, but should instead respond courageously. Lutzer further instructed followers of Christ to "be Gospel driven in your life and witness" (248; Mark 16:15; John 14:6); "do not bow to the culture's sexual revolution" (250; Matt. 5:8; John 17:17); and "love Jesus passionately and suffer well" (257; Matt. 24:12; John 14:15; 1 John 2:15–17; James 4:4).

Therefore, biblical stewards proclaim the truth that knowing God more intimately must be the greatest, highest, and most passionate desire of a follower of Jesus because intimacy is His idea and His greatest desire for all His people. Biblical stewards proclaim the truth that it is only in an intimate relationship with God, through Jesus Christ in the power of the Holy Spirit, that we discover our true identity and find meaning and purpose in life as His stewards. Biblical stewards proclaim the truth that a deeper walk with Jesus changes everything: it heals us, it

A CALL TO ACTION

restores us, it reconciles us, it comforts us, it encourages us, it calls us, it equips us, and it transforms us.

Biblical Stewards Sound a Clarion Call to the Body of Christ, the Church

As image bearers of God through Jesus Christ, we were created for a whole, meaningful relationship with God through our identity in Christ. Therefore, biblical stewards call to the body of Christ to steward this relationship by returning to His embrace, becoming so surrendered to Christ that His sweet aroma will flow from us and will draw all people to Him. "You are the salt of the earth, but if the salt loses its flavor, how shall it be seasoned?" (Matt. 5:13). "Ye are the light of the world. A city that is set on a hill cannot be hidden. Nor do we light a lamp and put it under a basket but on a lampstand and it gives light to all who are in the house. Let your light so shine before men that they may see your good works and glorify your Father in heaven" (Matt. 5:14–16). Biblical stewards call to the body of Christ to name the things that distract and pull us away from the intimacy God desires for us and surrender them back to God, thirsting for Him to take us to a deeper level than we've ever experienced, starting with confession and repentance. Biblical stewards call to the body of Christ to preach and teach against our works-focused culture and to proclaim the truth that abiding in Christ is our highest calling and God's greatest desire for our life. This is how we act as salt and light to those around us. The world needs

OUR RELATIONSHIP WITH GOD

what we have—a deep, growing, and abiding relationship with God through faith in His Son, Jesus Christ! The world needs the gospel! "But thanks be to God, who always leads us as captives in Christ's triumphal procession and uses us to spread the aroma of the knowledge of Him everywhere" (2 Cor. 2:14).

OUR RELATIONSHIP WITH SELF

Howard Rich

Therefore, if anyone is in Christ, that person is a new creation: The old has gone, the new is here!
—2 Corinthians 5:17

What We Believe about the Stewardship of Our Relationship to Self

We were created to be faithful stewards, and this stewardship extends to our relationship with ourselves. We do not own this relationship but steward it on behalf of the One who created us for it. As creations made in the image of God and objects of His love, we have been endowed with the gift of a conscience. This conscience allows us to know and comprehend the difference between right and wrong, having the ability to perceive reality beyond ourselves.

A CALL TO ACTION

Our understanding of self must come from God, for He tells us we are "fearfully and wonderfully made" (Ps. 139:14), and we belong to Him. He promises that "neither death nor life, neither angels nor demons, neither the present nor the future, nor any powers, neither height nor depth, nor anything else in all creation, will be able to separate us from the love of God that is in Christ Jesus" (Rom. 8:38). Genesis 1:27 states that God "created human beings in His own image. In the image of God He created them; male and female He created them." We are image bearers of a loving God.

Our self-identity is best understood within our relationship with God as His stewards. We have been created for a purpose, having a reason for being that extends beyond our mere existence in the universe. Together with all human beings, we have the ability to know God and glorify Him with our thoughts, words, and actions. As individuals, the intentional stewardship of those thoughts, words, and actions both honors our Creator and brings us the greatest satisfaction and personal meaning.

Have you ever used a little laser light to play with a cat? Cats will chase that little light all over a room, and even try to climb up a wall to catch the tiny spot created by the concentrated beam of light. As a young Christian in my early teens, I had a distorted and frustrating image of God's will. I was constantly chasing God's will, as if He was shining a spotlight on a specific area of the ground, and as soon as I would run to it, He would move

OUR RELATIONSHIP WITH SELF

the light. All I wanted to do was get under that light so I could be right smack in the center of His will. It took me quite some time to understand that God's will isn't a mysterious moving target that He keeps me running after.

As I grow in my understanding of God's will for me as His steward, I am constantly reminded that freedom draws the steward to renewed and necessary attention to personal devotion and prayer. Scripture and prayer are the conduits to the steward's understanding of how the Creator wants His resources deployed; God's will for His people and resources is found in Scripture and prayer. Without this incredible connection to God, we can experience spiritual paralysis as we wonder what we should do with what has been entrusted to our care.

We are "God's workmanship, created in Christ Jesus to do good works, which God prepared in advance for us to do" (Eph. 2:10). Paul reminds us in 1 Corinthians 1:26 to "think of what you were when you were called.". Men are not called due to their wisdom, their talents, or their status and stature. God calls out of His strength and provision. Paul points to the believer's responsibility to steward God's call in Ephesians 4:1, as He motivates us "to walk in a manner worthy of the calling with which [we] have been called."

Romans 12:2 reads, "And do not be conformed to this world, but be transformed by the renewing of your mind, so that you may prove what the will of God is, that which is good and acceptable and perfect." In this

A CALL TO ACTION

passage, Paul unveils the fact that disciples are to present themselves to God as a living sacrifice, unblemished, holy, and suitable before Him. These two verses (Rom. 12:2; Eph. 4:1) are calls to transformation for the disciple; what was is no longer; therefore, the believer is something new. The words in these verses describe a new creature that looks different and stands in contrast to the blemished and unacceptable offerings to God.

The believer must rely on Jesus, who walked through more than we can imagine. On the night before His trial and crucifixion, He came to terms with what it meant to empty Himself and drink from the cup of agony, sorrow, and wrath.

Jesus was deeply grieved as He prayed to His father in the Garden of Gethsemane (Matt. 26:36–56; Mark 14:32–52; Luke 22:40–53). He told the three disciples with Him, "My soul is very sorrowful, even to death" (Mark 14:34), and Luke tells us Jesus was in such agony that "His sweat became like great drops of blood falling to the ground" (Luke 22:44). Jesus's prayer to the Father was one of emptying Himself and accepting back from the Father a tremendous responsibility. In that garden Jesus asked the Father, "If it be possible, let this cup pass from me," but He immediately submitted to the Father by praying, "Nevertheless, not as I will, but as you will" (Matt. 26:39).

Stewardship is an ongoing cycle of recognition, relinquishing, and receiving; it is a tremendous act of moment-by-moment obedience and submission that

OUR RELATIONSHIP WITH SELF

requires continual alignment with the will of the Father. This cycle can be difficult and painful at times but is necessary and brings freedom.

Making good stewardship decisions can be difficult and stressful, but the good news is that we don't need to wander around in the darkness, because God sets His agenda in Scripture. What He wants us to do and how He wants us to interact with His creation is communicated through the history of salvation written in the Bible. God is constantly asking us to learn from His Scriptures and to bring our concerns to Him in prayer.

Freedom is found in the fact that God owns all creation and wants us to continually ask Him how to employ His possessions for His use. We don't have to worry about how to create resources, but we do need to know what to do with what comes into our care. There is a huge responsibility there, and it should drive us to our knees.

When we see ourselves as caretakers, we discover a wonderful truth: there is incredible freedom in being a steward as opposed to being an owner. The steward is free from the tyranny and encumbrances that come from striving after possessions but is obligated to understand the intentions of the Creator when resources are placed in his care. Stewardship necessitates dependence on the One who is the true Owner and frees the believer to respond in joyful worship.

As mortal human beings with immortal souls, our identity as created stewards gives us a profound sense of

A CALL TO ACTION

freedom and purpose far beyond the constraints of our molecular, physical bodies. Our dynamic relationship with God, along with a rich mix of influence from family, community, environment, belief, and experience, shapes this identity over time. This identity defines our role of cultivating everything God has given us and highlights the significance of His image being a part of our human nature. Reflecting God's image is inextricably connected to our meaning and purpose as persons.

The Parable of the Talents in Matthew 25 teaches the principle of stewardship and the inescapable fact that nothing belongs to a person that has not been entrusted to him by the rightful Owner. God is the Originator of everything in existence, He grants access to His resources at His discretion, and He has never abdicated His ownership. That is why our identity as stewards is so important and freeing. If we are not owners, we are free to stand with our hands open.

Early Christians understood that ownership rights were a primary competitor with Jesus for lordship in their lives. They modeled the way in service to Jesus because they understood that "No one can serve two masters. Either you will hate the one and love the other, or you will be devoted to the one and despise the other" (Matt. 6:24). It is through this understanding of lordship that Christian stewards can joyfully submit ownership issues to Jesus and experience a transformation in their identity in Him.

One of the biggest barriers to overcome on the

OUR RELATIONSHIP WITH SELF

journey to living as a steward is the idea of ownership. A Christian's calling is to fall under the lordship and Kingdom of Christ; however, if we are easily seduced and drawn into setting ourselves up as owners, we fall into a trap of rights, entitlements, and privileges. Despite our hope and desire to give Jesus total lordship, we hold certain things back, creating a barrier between us and Christ.

Being set free from an ownership mentality allows the believer to engage the world without regard to personal desires that may be contrary to God's purposes. Joyfully submitting to God's complete ownership begins the transformation of our identity as stewards. Our perspective changes from seeing ourselves as owners to seeing ourselves as caretakers. This release of ownership sets the believer free to fully rely on God's direction.

Our role as stewards is distinctive because it defines our relationship with God; it is our identity in Him. It also requires a complete dependence on God for every decision and action as His representatives. Stewardship speaks to the core of who we are in relation to God and His creation. Seeing ourselves as stewards instead of owners requires a change of perspective that will affect the meaning of our lives. If we embrace the identity of a steward, it will change every interaction we have, especially our relationship with God and ourselves.

This is why we must have an ongoing, vital, and personal relationship with Christ. It is that relationship with Him that allows us to surrender ownership, serve others,

A CALL TO ACTION

and shepherd our followers. Freedom from ownership helps us see our need for personal devotion and prayer. Scripture and prayer are the conduits to understanding how Jesus wants our lives deployed for Him.

When we view our role as a steward, we can see the position we occupy is not ours; it is Christ's, and we only do His bidding. However, when we do not live from a core identity as created stewards, we allow false narratives to define us. One lie tells us our identity is predetermined by the voices around us, including culture, gender, family, tradition, government, or tribe. The value of a person, when finding its root outside of God, shifts with those changeable voices, never finding a firm foundation of constant truth. This leads to relativism— truth shifts depending on the beliefs of these voices. it is an ever-moving target that our God-given conscience must constantly struggle to define.

A second deception is that we determine our own source of identity, that no other person or thing has any greater right in determining who we are than we ourselves. With this mindset, there is no other, larger, or spiritual first cause to whom we are subservient. Self-determination sets us up to trust in our limited human ability to direct our own path and destiny.

In contrast to the lie of self-determination, another narrative says we have no control at all over our self-identity, but that we are simply the product of material evolution; we are no different in fundamental substance from anything else in the natural world. We must accept

OUR RELATIONSHIP WITH SELF

our fate as being the result of a natural, biological process—the chance meeting of mutant cells throughout history. This belief leaves us devalued and hopeless in the deepest part of our being.

Therefore, biblical stewards reject the lie that we can find our identity and purpose in any other place than in an intimate relationship with God through Jesus Christ. We reject the lie that we control and determine our own identity, whether we (a) tie it to our success, achievements, or the roles we play, or (b) listen to the many voices that claim that our identity is a preference we choose for our own pleasure. Furthermore, biblical stewards reject the lie that our life, including our identity, belongs to us and not to God.

Biblical Stewards Are Committed to Proclaiming the Truth of the Gospel

As stewards, we proclaim the truth that, in Jesus Christ, the sin that seeks to rob us of our identity is overcome, that we are now children of God in Jesus Christ, and that this identity is a gift from God that we steward for His glory. As people reconciled to God, we are set free to follow Him wherever He calls, not seeking to build our reputation or gain the applause of others, but content to live in the will of God and enjoy the applause of nail-scarred hands. "For those who are led by the Spirit of God are the children of God. The Spirit you received does not make you slaves, so that you live in fear again; rather, the Spirit you received brought about your

A CALL TO ACTION

adoption to sonship. And by Him we cry, 'Abba, Father'" (Rom. 8:14–15). As stewards of this precious gift, we are called to the highest level of love and service, acting as champions of reconciliation and justice because all bear His image.

Biblical Stewards Sound a Clarion Call to the Body of Christ, the Church

As image bearers of God through Jesus Christ, we were created for whole, meaningful relationships with God through our identity in Christ. Therefore, biblical stewards call the body of Christ to stand firm against the lie that identity is self-defined and against the popular cultural narratives about human self-image that conflict with God's truth, and to affirm that every believer can find their identity as a child of God in Jesus Christ. Biblical stewards call the body of Christ to be compassionate toward all people because they are also made in God's image, and to fulfill its stewardship role by inviting all people to find their meaning, purpose, and identity in Christ. Biblical stewards call the body of Christ to preach, teach, and model the joy of knowing who we are because we know whose we are, and to experience the abundant life that Christ promised all who find their true identity in Him.

OUR RELATIONSHIP WITH OTHERS

Andrea Leigh Capuyan

Jesus replied: "Love the Lord your God with all your heart and with all your soul and with all your mind." This is the first and greatest commandment. And the second is like it: "Love your neighbor as yourself."
—Matthew 22:37–39

What We Believe about the Stewardship of Our Relationship with Others

With the two commands mentioned in Matthew 22:37–39, Jesus stipulates the daily life practice of His faithful stewards. Orthodox faith is expressed in the practice of love—love of God and love of others. And Jesus links our relationship with God and with self to our relationship with others, framing these relationships as intertwined and interdependent. Love of others is a natural outflow from the worship and love of God.

A CALL TO ACTION

Jesus's invitation begins with a call to relinquish our full self (heart, soul, and mind) to His care. We attune to God. We seek to be under His care, totally dependent on Him and fully vulnerable before Him. It is a relinquishment of self-sufficiency and self-centeredness. This place of relinquishment mirrors Jesus's example: "Have this mind among yourselves, which is yours in Christ Jesus, who, though He was in the form of God, did not count equality with God a thing to be grasped, but emptied Himself, by taking the form of a servant, being born in the likeness of men" (Phil. 2:5–7). Faithful stewards cannot practice the love of others without adopting a posture of "emptying" oneself before God, because it cultivates humility and an open heart receptive to God.

Security is a deep and fundamental need of every human being (Koch 2005). When God becomes our secure foundation, we are grounded in reality and able to respond to the community around us. Our trust in God becomes the anchor that allows us to trust others and to be trustworthy. This is the bedrock for human beings to experience secure attachment with others, because in God, our need for relationship, community, and belonging finds roots. Belonging is another universal need of every human that flourishes when there is a foundation of trust and security in God (Koch 2005). Fostering thriving relationships, building welcoming communities, offering a haven of safety, and having compassion are necessary for cultivating a sense of belonging and loving others well.

OUR RELATIONSHIP WITH OTHERS

Human beings were created to live and flourish in relationship with one another. This is a central theme in the creation story in Genesis and of God's intended design. Communion with one another is an expression of the triune God. We are not singular image bearers of the likeness of God. Bearing the image and likeness of God is fully expressed in the Church body, in followers of Jesus Christ, who span across history and around the globe. God's kingdom is a community—a body. Stewards are called to be builders of the community, though sin, selfishness, and corruption have distorted and destroyed God's intended design for human relationships. The Church indwelt by the Spirit of Christ is God's gift to restore and renew what sin has broken. Faithful stewards are also entrusted to bring restoration and renewal to the life of a community.

The words of Isaiah provide a vision for this renewal: "…and you shall be like a watered garden, like a spring of water, whose waters do not fail. And your ancient ruins shall be rebuilt; you shall raise the foundations of many generations; you shall be called the repairer of the breach, the restorer of streets to dwell in" (Isa. 58:11–12). This picture for God's people is in the context of worship. Earlier in chapter 58, the prophet contrasts the practice of those who are focused on true worship with those who feign love for God. This contrast is centered around the love and care of others. Isaiah reminds the people that God desires faithful worship that includes caring for those who are in need as well as championing

A CALL TO ACTION

justice and mercy for the oppressed. The mindset of the faithful steward embraces the role as God's trusted agent, serving His kingdom as a protector and healer. This image of God's people repairing "ancient ruins" is referenced again in Isaiah 61:1–4, a powerful passage of hope and healing in the lives of God's people:

> The Spirit of the Lord God is upon me, because the Lord has anointed me to bring good news to the poor; He has sent me to bind up the brokenhearted, to proclaim liberty to the captives, and the opening of the prison to those who are bound; to proclaim the year of the Lord's favor, and the day of vengeance of our God; to comfort all who mourn; to grant to those who mourn in Zion—to give them a beautiful headdress instead of ashes, the oil of gladness instead of mourning, the garment of praise instead of a faint spirit; that they may be called oaks of righteousness, the planting of the Lord, that He may be glorified. They shall build up the ancient ruins; they shall raise the former devastations; they shall repair the ruined cities, the devastations of many generations.

In this message of freedom and healing to individuals, notice how these mighty "oaks" become a display of the Lord God's work and become agents who restore devastated communities. Personal transformation in Christ frees us to faithfully steward healing in our communities

OUR RELATIONSHIP WITH OTHERS

and relationships. As God rescues, redeems, and renews us, we are released to impact and be impacted by others. It is a beautiful picture of the steward serving God's kingdom as a change agent for the restoration and peace of the people.

Our lives are defined by a multitude of relationships that are multifaceted and layered. Most of us are sons, daughters, friends, family, neighbors, citizens, Christians, and the list goes on. It is overlapping circles of relationship that the steward navigates through daily life in communion with others. Daily life in God's kingdom is an opportunity for the faithful steward to serve as emissary and ambassador, declaring the freedom and healing our good God offers. Stewards actively consider their impact and practice of love within their relationships, defined as (a) family and friendships, (b) communal life within the Church and the neighborhood, (c) ethnic and cultural affinities, and (d) societal participation and citizenship. These circles of relationship represent the roles and intersections of relationships that expand from us. These are concentric circles that reflect varying degrees of intimacy, affinity, and depth. In all these spaces and all these relationships, we steward caregiving. We steward justice, compassion, and mercy—the healing of the nations.

Humility defines this practice of love. It is in full recognition of our limitations and of our blind spots that we can guard against deceptions that impair our ability to steward our relationship with others. Humility requires that the faithful steward maintain a posture

A CALL TO ACTION

of reflection, willing to learn from God and others. This posture positions the steward to examine lies and obstacles that undermine creating good and loving relationships. Only with humility and honesty can the steward engage in meaningful relationships that foster restoration, freedom, and goodness. True intimacy, affinity, and depth are experienced in the context of humble and honest relationships.

Sadly, sin created separation from God and segregation among humanity. Sin divides what God has designed to be in communion. Sin is at the heart of all that separates us from our neighbors and causes us to see others as the enemy. Looking back to the story of Adam and Eve in the Garden of Eden, isolation, blame, and division are evident. God's design for mutual communion, human flourishing, community, and belonging is severed and shattered. Idolatry, selfishness, and greed seed an ownership mentality that prohibits the practice of love because our commitment to self-centeredness leads to violence. It is there at the very beginning of Genesis. One of the first stories outside of God's good garden is the tragic story of Cain and Abel, in which a brother turns on his brother, resulting in bloodshed.

In his book *Playing God: Redeeming the Gift of Power*, Andy Crouch (2013) highlighted the distortion caused by sin that is at the root of human conflict and division. Humanity rejected our role to bear God's image as we were designed, and instead chose to create an idol in its image. This idolatry of "the self" corrupts the

OUR RELATIONSHIP WITH OTHERS

gift of power God gives humanity for fruitfully living together—for growing together and expanding goodness and beauty together. This idolatry leads to the violent domination of others and the commitment to create a human "empire" in competition with the rule of the kingdom of God. This blind pursuit of personal "empire-building" is a modern-day addiction that breaks relationships across all the concentric circles of the community we experience in life.

Faithful stewards reject the concept of allegiance to any empire above or equal to our allegiance to the kingdom of God. Stewarding our relationships requires a commitment to reject the "us" and "them" mentality. Instead, stewards actively pursue bridging differences through compassion and curiosity, and are committed to treating all people as unique image bearers of God. We all face challenges of internal bias and stereotypes of the "other." Courageous stewards confront personal notions of prejudice and bias, asking God to remove any personal barriers that impede us from building up others and a devotion to His kingdom.

There is another temptation that inhibits our ability to love others. Far too often we view other people as commodities, so we define the value of our relationships based on our benefit. It is a lie to deem other people and our connection with them as valuable if they serve our happiness. It is a lie to control others to ensure our satisfaction and self-preservation. We reject the utilitarian temptation to reduce the value of our interpersonal

A CALL TO ACTION

relationships to something akin to quid pro quo. To hold this view rejects human dignity. Instead, it is a perverted view that sees other individuals as objects to be acquired, controlled, and owned. The danger is that this mindset leads to exploitation because our relationships are weighed for our benefit and gain (Crouch 2016). Fear of losing our foothold or position gives way to oppression, and we become agents of totalitarianism in our home, church, work, friendships, and every other area of our life. This exploitation is evident in dysfunctional codependency in relationships where we feed off the needs of others. It is evident in our unhealthy obsession with celebrity and fame, thriving on "likes," flattery, and attention. Faithful stewards understand that God designed our relationships for mutual flourishing—the giving and receiving of respect, help, and love. In our relationships with others, we are invited to honor another's best interest above our own. We offer care and concern, acknowledging our own vulnerability and that we too need other people.

God intends for us to experience intimacy in our relationship with others. That is a full expression of hospitality and communion, and it is unique to our experience with other human beings as compared to our relationship with the rest of creation. Depth and authenticity cultivate meaning. It is impossible to develop meaningful relationships without presence, selflessness, patience, repentance, and sacrifice. To remain resistant to reflection and confession is to entertain notions of

OUR RELATIONSHIP WITH OTHERS

superiority and superficiality. We set ourselves above others and give way to the temptation to view others as inferior to us.

Paul exhorted Christians in Rome to behave differently: "Therefore, let us not pass judgment on one another any longer, but rather decide never to put a stumbling block or hindrance in the way of a brother" (Rom. 14:13). In this portion of Paul's letter, he provided a broader vision for Christian behavior—to move toward others even amid disagreement. Faithful stewards will adopt an inviting and welcoming attitude, listening to the concerns of others rather than avoiding or dismissing them. We reject the temptation to promote agendas—personal, political, or religious. Instead, we engage others as ministers of reconciliation, that is, a life of forgiveness and freedom found in Jesus Christ our Lord. In doing so, we steward our relationships with others through this guiding principle: "So then let us pursue what makes for peace and mutual upbuilding" (Rom. 14:19).

The temptations of idolatry, exploitation, and arrogance obstruct the Christ-centered stewarding of relationships and the care of our communities. These present dangers cause us to manipulate and control others, creating hurt, division, and isolation. This is not how God designed us to bear His image as individuals and the corporate body of Christ. To practice love, to be agents of justice and mercy, to be ministers of reconciliation, we must adopt an attitude that is committed to

A CALL TO ACTION

humility. God invites us to confess and release any attitude or motivation that prevents the Holy Spirit's work to transform us into Christ's image and likeness. Faithful stewards embrace this transformation, welcoming the changes God makes in our hearts that move us toward others in a spirit of forgiveness and kindness.

Biblical Stewards Are Committed to Proclaiming the Truth of the Gospel

As faithful stewards, we are called to pursue reconciliation through compassion and engagement with others, committing to treat all people as unique image bearers of God. Healthy, loving relationships with others require mutual respect. Forgiveness requires us to name every sin that keeps us divided. True reconciliation means we repent of every attitude that separates us, and we boldly steward every opportunity to honor God through loving our neighbor as He commanded. Loving others as yourself puts you in the role of a helper, ally, and advocate. Only when we stop controlling relationships to serve our interests can we bless others as we follow Jesus. Loving others well invites relationships that are interdependent, where giving and receiving take place equally. Stewards acknowledge personal limitations and reject an attitude of independence and arrogance; rather, we affirm that we are made whole by the love of Christ. This sets us free to respond to care for the best interests of others above our own desires. We acknowledge that we cannot control any person, yet each of us can impact the trajectory of another person's life. A life of impact invites stewards to invest deeply in others, avoiding transactional relationships. Instead, we recognize the value of every human life as created and deeply loved by God.

Biblical Stewards Sound a Clarion Call to the Body of Christ, the Church

Jesus prayed that we might be one as He and the Father are one, for then the world will "know that you sent me and have loved them even as you have loved me" (John 17:21–23). This is a holy calling for stewards. When we accept an invitation to repair broken walls, we move into a life of stewarding this holy calling to display the love of God to others. Living in this calling results in the body of Christ preaching boldly against the sins that divide us, repenting, and raising a new vision for the relationships that God has placed in our care, in the communities in which we will live and participate. This vision is our commitment to the promised fulfillment of Jesus's prayer that God's will be accomplished on earth as it is in heaven. The steward whose focus is God's kingdom lives with a transcendent mindset, stewarding every relationship with an eye toward eternity. Stewards accept the call to be the loudest voice seeking biblical justice for our neighbor, the first person to seek forgiveness and reconciliation. We are called to a steadfast, dedicated tenacity committed to a lifelong journey to learn and a willingness to grow and change, allowing God to remove any resistance within us. We are called to preach against

A CALL TO ACTION

our "ownership" attitudes regarding our relationships. We are committed to letting God set us free to love our neighbor through Jesus Christ for the sake of the witness of the Church and the transformation of our culture.

As stewards, we are challenged to love in each of these relationships as we love ourselves, we are challenged to give of ourselves as Christ demonstrated for us, and we are challenged to see our family, our neighbors, and our communities as Christ does. In his letter to the Ephesians, Paul inspires us to consider this great work and call that God has prepared for us: a calling that moves beyond human identities, which create inequalities and divisions—a calling rooted in the unity found in Christ. This is Paul's prayer, that followers of Christ be "grounded in love" for one another. It is through this vision and this hope that we move forward, trusting that God can "do far more abundantly than all that we ask or think, according to the power at work within us" (Eph. 3:20). Let us live in our communities in this call of unity from Paul, believing that God is at work in our lives and the lives of others for His glory and fame.

> *"My prayer is not for them alone. I pray also for those who will believe in me through their message, that all of them may be one, Father, just as you are in me and I am in you. May they also be in us so that the world may believe that you have sent me."*
>
> —John 17:20–21

OUR RELATIONSHIP WITH CREATION

Dr. Ben Porter

The earth is the Lord's, and everything in it, the world, and all who live in it.

—PSALM 24:1

What We Believe About the Stewardship of Our Relationship with Creation

We were created to be faithful stewards, which includes our relationship with creation. According to Genesis 1:26–27, God made mankind in His image. This distinction comes with responsibility in the subsequent verses as God places mankind as a steward for His creation, stating in Genesis 1:28: "Be fruitful and increase in number; fill the earth and subdue it. Rule over the fish in the sea and the birds in the sky and over every living creature that moves on the ground." The concept

A CALL TO ACTION

of stewardship hinges on the relationship between an owner and a steward. We do not own this relationship, but we steward it on behalf of the One who created this world for us. We read in Psalm 24:1 that "The earth is the Lord's, and everything in it, the world, and all who live in it." We are not called to be owners of earth. We are called to be stewards for the Lord, the Owner of all things, representing His interests in our dominion of the earth. Part of our call in stewarding our relationship with God involves stewarding our relationship with creation and the resources He puts in our care.

The interpretation of the term "dominion," found in the King James Version of Genesis, has long been a point of contention. As mankind has continued to claim ownership of earth, "dominion" has been redefined as "domination." Carefree use and abuse of the natural world has taken the place of the careful consideration of resources both for today and for future generations. For the steward leader, the term "dominion" can only be accurately defined by God, the Creator and Redeemer of the world. The purpose of the dominion given to mankind is for peace and the blessings that God intends for us and all creatures. We see in 1 Kings 10:9 that God established kings to "maintain justice and righteousness." God's definition of an ideal king in the Old Testament is founded in the benefits for those under the king's care. With this understanding, it is impossible to conclude that God's mandate to mankind means that we can use creation however we would like. Instead, our decisions

OUR RELATIONSHIP WITH CREATION

as stewards of creation must align with God's purposes and values.

A biblical understanding of creation establishes the value of nature. Everything that is in the world today has come from the combination of mankind and the Garden of Eden. Looking at all that He had made, God stated in Genesis 1:31 that "it was very good." Understanding the value that God has for creation aligns believers with His value of the created world. We are called to value the things that He sees as valuable, including the created natural world. Christianity, more than any other religion, gives us a reason to be passionate about protecting the earth. In Psalm 19:3–4, David described creation and the natural world, stating, "They have no speech, they use no words; no sound is heard from them. Yet their voice goes out into all the earth, their words to the ends of the world…" God continues to use creation as a means of general revelation. Romans 1:20 states, "For since the creation of the world God's invisible qualities—His eternal power and divine nature—have been clearly seen, being understood from what has been made, so that people are without excuse." Creation has value because God places value on it and because it allows mankind to see the nature of God through His works.

Nowhere are the competing loyalties for our hearts more clearly seen than in our relationship with creation. Oftentimes, if not most times, well-planned buildings, including those for ministry purposes, are budgeted for

A CALL TO ACTION

and built with little regard to environmental impact or sustainable design options. While these are not always intentional decisions or omissions, the lack of consideration can often be traced to perceived ownership on the part of the builder. Within the Church we have seen a spirit of ownership and control produce a compromised message that comingles kingdom values with worldly principles, which ultimately places God's people in bondage. How we view our relationship to time, talents, finances, and the earth itself has a powerful impact on our life and witness as the Church of Jesus Christ. In their book *Creation Care*, Douglas Moo and Jonathan Moo (2018) stated that Christians should be involved in actively caring for creation for the following reasons: (a) the need to address current environmental challenges, (b) to serve as a witness in our time, and (c) the witness of Scripture to the importance of our vocation as keepers of creation. Unfortunately, we have bought into the lie of the enemy that we own what only God owns and control what is His alone. As stewards, we must reject these lies with the full force of God's truth.

In *The Nature of Environmental Stewardship*, Johnny Wei-Bing Lin (2016) recognized that caring for creation should be part of believers' worship of God, our relationship of love with God, and our responsibility to God as image bearers and stewards. As steward leaders, we are called to steward our relationship with God, ourselves, our neighbors, and creation. By appropriately stewarding our relationship with creation, we are thereby able to

OUR RELATIONSHIP WITH CREATION

demonstrate stewardship of our relationship with God, ourselves, and also our neighbors.

We steward our relationship with God, in part, through caring for creation. Recognizing and understanding the will of God for the natural world allows us to make decisions that align with His purposes. Understanding that we are not owners, but stewards, is freeing and provides for us a framework for decision making as it relates to the use of our resources. It is through prayer and the study of Scripture that the steward understands the value God places on creation and the responsibility that goes with making decisions on His behalf.

We steward our relationship with ourselves, in part, by caring for creation. As creations made in the image of God, we have been given a conscience and the ability to perceive right from wrong. With this comes the ability to distinguish past and present decisions as being right or wrong through self-examination. This understanding allows us to correct and redirect our decisions to better align with the will of God. As we consider how to care for creation, we must examine how our decisions will impact the world today, as well as the generations to come.

We steward our relationships with our neighbors, in part, through caring for creation. The ability to care for the earth on God's behalf belongs as much to the generations that follow us as it does to us today. Therefore, we would be foolish to think that our decisions only impact current generations. The depletion of resources or the extinction

A CALL TO ACTION

of species prevents future generations from having the same opportunities or experiencing the same beauty we do. "Sustainability" can be defined as living today with an understanding that tomorrow will come. It is our responsibility as believers to steward creation and a way forward that demonstrates love for current and future generations.

Therefore, biblical stewards reject the lie that God is not concerned with how we use and invest our time, our skills, or our money and that the Church has no right to talk about them or challenge how we steward them. Biblical stewards reject the lie that the earth will be destroyed at the end of the age, so it is not worth caring for now—that the biblical teaching on dominion gives us license to abuse, destroy, or wantonly disregard creation, and that God's only goal is salvation of the soul—denying our full stewardship responsibility. Furthermore, biblical stewards reject the lie of the so-called prosperity gospel that God has granted creation to humanity in its entirety and that material blessings are the entitlement of believers.

Biblical Stewards Are Committed to Proclaiming the Truth of the Gospel

As stewards, we view all of life as a gift, and our purpose in life is to steward it faithfully on behalf of God, the true Owner. It is from our foundation as God's stewards that we are called for further purposes. Whether leaders or followers, we are first stewards, responsible for all that God has put into our care, including our time, our skills, our money, and our natural resources.

OUR RELATIONSHIP WITH CREATION

In Matthew 25:14–30, Jesus teaches that stewards have an obligation to the owner's interests and that stewards will be judged based on the return gained on those interests. It is not the decision of the steward as to the amount he receives; instead, that is the prerogative of the master. It is the master's *right* to give as he sees fit. However, it is the *responsibility* of the steward to ensure a return on what he has been given. Through the teachings in Scripture, it is clear that God, as the Owner, deals in the realm of rights, whereas we, as stewards, deal in the realm of responsibility.

Therefore, biblical stewards proclaim the truth that our use of every second of time, every ounce of our abilities, and every penny God has entrusted to us is a stewardship issue that requires prayer, discernment, and obedience; thus, instruction on how we steward them is the right, proper, and essential work of the Church. Biblical stewards proclaim the truth that we are commanded and called to treat creation as God's gift to us, to use it as God intended it to be used, and that "dominion" means protecting, caring for, conserving, and sustaining God's creation as His representatives, guardians, and stewards. Biblical stewards also proclaim the truth that God is a God of abundance and He has entrusted His people with the resources needed to fully fund every vision, goal, and plan He places in the hearts of the leaders of His churches, ministries, and organizations—"pressed down, shaken together and overflowing" (Luke 6:38).

A CALL TO ACTION

Biblical Stewards Sound a Clarion Call to the Body of Christ, the Church

As image bearers of God through Jesus Christ, we were created for whole, meaningful relationships with God through our identity in Christ. As stewards, we must respond obediently to Scripture's clear command to steward creation in all its forms that will bear witness to the world of the Lordship of Jesus Christ over all things. For too long, Christians have recognized God as Creator but have failed to care for His creation.

In *Redeeming Creation: The Biblical Basis for Environmental Stewardship*, Van Dyke et al. (1996) recognized the dearth of sermons and Sunday school lessons on environmental themes, despite the integral part they play in the biblical message. Pastors have not only an opportunity, but a responsibility to emphasize the biblical view of creation in worship and instruction. Additionally, Van Dyke et al. stated that pastors and church leaders modeling attitudes of commitment is highly important. With growing opportunities for building sustainably designed structures, churches should also consider how building projects can be used as a means of stewarding creation.

Therefore, as biblical stewards, we call the body of Christ to preach boldly that our security and our identity are found only in Jesus Christ and not in material things, freeing God's people to an unprecedented level of lavish generosity that reflects the abundance of God and equips His work globally for such a time as this. We call the body of Christ to preach and live out the whole

OUR RELATIONSHIP WITH CREATION

gospel and the message of hope and reconciliation to a broken world, to seek intimacy with God as our highest calling, and to not allow the pursuit, accumulation, or false security of money to usurp the place of God in our hearts and lives. We call the body of Christ to care for the environment by loving God through valuing the things He loves and by seeking the well-being and flourishing of all aspects of creation.

> *Let all creation rejoice before the LORD, for He comes, He comes to judge the earth. He will judge the world in righteousness and the peoples in His faithfulness.*
> —PSALM 96:13

CONCLUSION

"Obedient and joyful response—that is the only requirement of the steward leader. However, for us to be true to this calling, to be consistent and unshakable in this one vocational focus, we must embrace a new paradigm for effective leadership. This paradigm emphasizes 'being' over 'doing' and 'freedom' over 'ownership.'" "Throughout Scripture, God 'called' leaders, asking only for their obedient response. He called many ill-equipped, untrained, dysfunctional, poorly skilled men and women into leadership. He thrust them into impossible situations with recalcitrant people and asked only that they be obedient and trusting. This is the posture of the…steward leader" (Rodin 2010, 55–56).

God, throughout history, has raised up devoted steward leaders like Joseph, Nehemiah, and Esther during times of crises to address problems His way. These leaders worked to faithfully fulfill the purposes of the Master, God, for all He had so graciously entrusted to their care. These resources included time, treasure, talent, and relationships. Leaders like Esther were selected for "such a

A CALL TO ACTION

time as this"! Will you be a steward leader who will not be silenced but will instead respond courageously to our culture's assault on Christianity? Lutzer's (2020) challenge to faithful steward leaders is to be gospel-driven in life and witness (Mark 16:15; John 14:6), to not bow to the culture's sexual revolution (Matt. 5:8; John 17:17), and to love Jesus passionately and suffer well (Matt. 224:12; John 14:15; James 4:4; 1 John 2:15–17). In Lutzer's words, "Engage the Culture and stand against it!" (261).

REFERENCES

Birch, Bruce C. 2002. "Leadership as Stewardship." *Quarterly Review* 22(4): 358–69.

Block, Peter. 2013. *Stewardship: Choosing Service over Self-Interest.* Berrett-Koehler Publishers, Inc.

Bridges, Jerry. 1996. *The Pursuit of Holiness.* NavPress.

Crouch, Andy. 2013. *Playing God: Redeeming the Gift of Power.* InterVarsity Press.

Crouch, Andy. 2016. *Strong and Weak: Embracing a Life of Love, Risk & True Flourishing.* InterVarsity Press.

Greenleaf, Robert K. 1977. *Servant Leadership: A Journey into the Nature of Legitimate Power and Greatness.* Paulist Press.

Hendricks, Howard. 1987. *Teaching to Change Lives.* Multnomah Press.

Koch, Kathy. 2005. *Finding Authentic Hope and Wholeness: 5 Questions That Will Change Your Life.* Moody Publishers.

Lin, Johnny Wei-Bing. 2016. *The Nature of Environmental Stewardship: Understanding Creation Care Solutions to Environmental Problems.* Pickwick Publications.

Lutzer, Erwin. 2020. *We Will Not Be Silenced: Responding Courageously to Our Culture's Assault on Christianity.* Harvest House.

A CALL TO ACTION

Moo, Douglas. J., and Moo, Jonathan. A. 2018. *Creation Care: A Biblical Theology of the Natural World.* Zondervan.

Nee, Watchman. 1979. *The Normal Christian Life.* Tyndale.

Rodin, R. Scott. 2013. *The Steward Leader: Transforming People, Organizations and Communities.* IVP Academic.

Van Dyke, Fred H., Mahan, David. C., Sheldon, Joseph. K., and Brand, Raymond. H. 1996. *Redeeming Creation: The Biblical Basis for Environmental Stewardship.* InterVarsity Press.

Veith, Gene. E. Jr. 2002. *God at Work: Your Christian Vocation in All of Life.* Crossway.

Willard, Dallas. 1998. *The Divine Conspiracy: Rediscovering Our Hidden Life in God.* HarperSanFrancisco.

Wilson, Kent R. 2016. *Steward Leadership in the Nonprofit Organization.* InterVarsity Press.

ABOUT THE AUTHORS

R. Scott Rodin

Over the past thirty-eight years Scott Rodin has helped hundreds of organizations improve their effectiveness in leadership, fund development, strategic planning, and board development. His work has impacted individuals, ministries and churches in the U.S., Canada, Middle East, Great Britain, China, Philippines, and Australia.

Dr. Rodin is Senior Consultant/Chief Strategy Officer for The Focus Group. He currently serves as a Senior Fellow of the Association of Biblical Higher Education and as board chair for ChinaSource. In addition, Dr. Rodin is past president of Eastern Baptist Theological Seminary, the Christian Stewardship Association, and Rodin Consulting, Inc., and he owns and operates Kingdom Life Publishing. He is a trainer and coach for the Board Training programs at ABHE and the Gianforte Family Foundation.

Dr. Rodin holds Master of Theology and Doctor of Philosophy degrees in Systematic Theology from the University of Aberdeen, Scotland. He's written seventeen books including *The Third Conversion, The Steward Leader,* and *The Four Gifts of the King.* He speaks regularly at conferences, retreats, and professional development events.

Scott is married to Linda, and they reside in Spokane, Washington.

Follow his blog at: www.thestewardsjourney.com

Order books or request for Dr. Rodin to speak at: www.kingdomlifepublishing.com

Dr. Brian S. Simmons, MS, EdD

Dr. Brian S. Simmons serves as associate provost and professor for CIU Global at Columbia International University. He is a board member for Ben Lippen School where he serves as the chair of the Governance Committee and a member of the Executive Committee, chair of the Harbour Watch Pool and Clubhouse Committee, and small group leader for Radius Church. He also serves as president of Nehemiah Group, LLC, which specializes in board training, executive coaching, and strategic planning. Dr. Simmons serves as the Scholar in residence for the Center for Steward Leader Studies.

Dr. Simmons is a graduate of Cornerstone University in Grand Rapids, Michigan, where he earned a Bachelor of Arts in Mathematics with a minor in biology. Dr. Simmons graduated summa cum laude and was recognized by the faculty for outstanding service to the institution in the divisions of science, social science, and education. He is also a graduate of Calvin College, earning a Bachelor of Science in Education. He earned a Master of Science in Education from Indiana University.

ABOUT THE AUTHORS

Finally, Dr. Simmons earned a Doctor of Education from Ball State University, where he was awarded the Dean's Citation for Academic Excellence. Additionally, Dr. Simmons earned his Certificate in Fundraising Management from the Fundraising School at Indiana University.

Dr. Simmons began his career as a mathematics teacher at Elkhart Christian Academy in Indiana, where he later served as superintendent for seven years. He served Heritage Christian School as superintendent for a decade, leading Heritage to grow from 1,180 to 1,650 students while overseeing a $17 million campus expansion project. He also served as an elder at College Park Church during that time. Later, Dr. Simmons was appointed as vice president of University Relations at Indiana Wesleyan University. Then, prior to his current role at CIU, Dr. Simmons was appointed as the fourth president of the Association of Christian Schools International, which is the largest Christian school association in the world.

Dr. Simmons serves as a visionary builder to further the kingdom of God through Christian education, teaching, and influencing others. His life verse is: "Seek ye first the kingdom of God and His righteousness and all these things shall be added unto you" (Matt. 6:33). He has been married to his wife, Bonnie, for forty-one years. He has four children (all married), and twelve grandchildren.

Dr. Simmons enjoys spending time with his wife and family, reading, boating, and outdoor activities.

STEWARD DECLARATION

Howard Rich, PhD

Howard is a lifelong advocate of generous living and desires to see Christians lead from a heart of stewardship and generosity. For sixteen years, Howard lived and worked in South Korea in the defense industry, during which time he earned a PhD in organizational leadership, concentrating on stewardship in for-profit businesses. He and his wife now live in Lancaster, Pennsylvania, where they both serve with international nonprofit organizations.

Andrea Leigh Capuyan, MA, CCNL, CNAP

Since 2007, Andrea Leigh Capuyan has served as the executive director of a local Christian ministry, the LPC, in Laurel, Maryland. The LPC is a local, grassroots agency providing practical help and counseling-based services for women and men facing unwanted, unsupported, and unintended pregnancies. The LPC also exists to provide a safe place of healing for those impacted by past abortion choices. The LPC team is centered on Christ, believing that God meets us in life's most challenging circumstances. In those situations, when we feel trapped or want to give up, God shows up through the kindness and compassion of His followers. The LPC team is an awesome testimony to the power and hope of the gospel of Jesus Christ, reminding us that our story isn't over and in situations of life and death, God resurrects and renews.

Andrea was drawn to The LPC because of her own story and because she cares deeply for women confronted

ABOUT THE AUTHORS

with unwanted pregnancies. She loves serving with the LPC team because they are willing to grapple with difficult realities yet hold hope in all situations.

Born and raised in Auburn, Alabama, Andrea has made the Washington, DC, area her home with her husband, Wayne, since 1996. Andrea holds a master's degree in organizational leadership from York College, and she is a graduate of world missions from Toccoa Falls College. She is a credentialed Christian nonprofit leader with the Christian Leadership Alliance, and she successfully completed the certified nonprofit accounting professional program with the organization, Nonprofit CPAs.

Andrea is passionate about developing leaders, cultivating healthy organizational culture, and fostering a collaborative management approach in teams. She especially enjoys working with other women who are in the midst of changing careers and vocations. For many years, Andrea has joined other thought leaders across the United States at the Steward Summit, where she has also presented about steward leadership. Andrea serves on the board of Center for Steward Leader Studies. She regularly writes about steward leadership topics for the Christian Leadership Alliance's *Higher Thinking* blog.

Andrea loves to cook, travel, and sing. She says, "Music moves me, and I love singing in a roomful of women in harmony." For Andrea, laughter, great conversation, and a warm cup of coffee are all ingredients for the perfect day!

STEWARD DECLARATION

Dr. Ben Porter, MEd, PhD

Dr. Ben Porter received his BA from The Citadel, The Military College of South Carolina. He earned an MEd and PhD from Columbia International University. His dissertation was entitled *Christian Educational Institution Leaders' Environmental Stewardship Belief and Its Impact on Campus and Construction Decisions*. He currently serves as the assistant head of school and lower school principal at Ben Lippen School in Columbia, South Carolina. He also serves as the executive director of the Crest Online, a Christian online high school. Ben is married to Margaret Porter and has two sons (Drake and Stone). In his spare time, he enjoys hunting, fishing, and exploring with his family.

ABOUT THE EDITOR

Susanna J. Spencer Wright

Susanna J. Spencer Wright is a writer and copy editor with a love for the written word. She has edited college papers, doctoral dissertations, scholarly research articles, manuscripts, curriculum, web content, and more.

Susanna currently serves Columbia International University as the lead dissertation stylist for the PhD in organizational leadership program with CIU Global, and serves as an editor with Good Comma Editing, based in Dayton, Ohio. She previously worked for Anderson University in Anderson, Indiana, as the content specialist for the Office of Marketing and Communication and worked in the same role for Indiana Wesleyan University in Marion, Indiana, before that.

Susanna loves to travel, read, run, watch documentaries, and spend quality time with her friends and family. She graduated from Indiana Wesleyan University in 2011 with bachelor's degrees in writing, leadership, and public relations, and currently resides in Marion, Indiana.

Made in United States
Orlando, FL
27 June 2024